CRUISING TO NIRVANA ON DREAMS

by

Dick Credit

"We are such stuff as dreams are made on,
And our little life is rounded with a sleep."

Prospero

A narrative tale told in poetry.

ISBN 0-9702336-0-4

Published by:

Love Extension Press
35 Holt Lane, Suite B
Chico, CA 95926

Cover Art by:

Titus Woods &
David Philhour

Dedication

To my life's partner
for committing to being
all that she is capable of being.
Without her mind,
guided by her heart,
this work would not have been possible.
For where two or more are gathered together,
in Love's name,
only then is there the power to create a perfect union
and enter, hand in hand, the Promised Land.
Of course being full of bosom,
narrow of waist, broad of hip,
and sturdy of thigh sweetens the pie.

ACKNOWLEDGEMENTS

Rudyard Kipling for:

"If you can dream--and not make dreams your master"

Moses for:

"God created man in his image and likeness."

Jesus for:
"What I have done all men can do and even more…
And greater things than these shall you do…
The Kingdom is within. and
To Love is the most important law."

Elizabeth Barrett Browning:

For telling me to Love to the depth and breadth
And height my soul can reach when feeling out of sight
For the ends of being and ideal grace.

Chief Seattle for telling me:

"Today you can see tomorrow."

William Henley for:

"I am the Captain of my soul."

Lao Tzu:

For teaching me The Way.

Omar Khayyam for:

"Ah Love! could thou and I with Fate conspire
To Grasp this sorry Scheme of Things entire,
Would not we shatter it to bits - and then
Re-mould it nearer to the Heart's Desire!"

Longfellow for:

"Tell me not in mournful numbers
life is but an empty dream.
For the soul is dead that slumbers
And things are not what they seem."

A Course In Miracles

For teaching me fear is the opposite of love
but when Love is all encompassing
it has no opposite.
And nothing real can be threatened,
nothing unreal exists.

The Goddess on my starboard lee
who taught me
Perfect Love conquers death.

Shakespeare for:

"This above all: to thine ownself be true,
And it must follow as the night the day,
Thou canst not then be false to any man."

FOREWORD

Dick Credit's poetry is to read and absorb because he's lived life on a grand scale. Not the grandiose pretensions and foppishness of the privileged, but an adventurous life of mythic dimension involving courage, great resolve and imagination in creating for himself a life apart.

The title poem is a touchstone for the book: As a young boy, Credit stood with his grandfather overlooking the Charles River in Boston; they talked about what life might have in store for one. Losing a parent early will kill or sharpen one's zest for life; the child Credit wasn't afraid to ask big questions. He was lucky in having a grandfather who spoke wisely, if in parable. And by his own courage, industry and imagination, and especially, by living a life based on every aspect of *love* he could comprehend, Credit's provided his own answers, which are the core of this magnificent book.

Almost every boy who's lived once dreamed of life at sea. Almost none of us ever got there, unless going to fight somebody's wars. Credit did live the sea life; he sailed a lot, then he sailed in boats he built. To me, "Shipwreck" is a great poem because of the story it tells; because of the grand language used to tell that story; and most of all, because that story is an utterly convincing account of a life based in love, compassion and humor as well as courage.

Sanford Dorbin, poet, bibliographer, editor

PREFACE

Professor Ronald Segal, a psychopharmacologist at UCLA, states in his book Intoxication *that science should recognize intoxication as a fourth instinct in humankind, along with sex, hunger and thirst.*

This poet's concept of a fourth instinct is not that of intoxication and its connotations, but that of experiencing bliss in one's own heart. If our dreams are truly attainable, then this narrative becomes a how-to book.

One can experience bliss with open mind and trust in the power of the mind. With nothing to lose and everlasting treasure to gain it's worth a try.
Why not?

Dick Credit

CONTENTS

INTRODUCTION

The heart engaging tale of making dreams come true
for the love of it.

Love is a mystery.
It baffles science.
To know Love,
the experience is necessary.

At times erotic.

I asked her,
"What do you want out of life?"

"If I can have that choice,
then I want everything."

"Everything is to be consumed
in the heat of loving passion,
to go beyond in Perfect Love.
To set sail on the seas
of everlasting bliss,
to dance with the Gods."

"Sounds like a plan..."

ON THE BANKS OF THE CHARLES
Early Thirties, The Great Depression

I remember, I remember the bar where I was born.
It was before school began when I was five.
A sunny spring afternoon strolling with Grampa,
the Irish one, along the banks of the Charles.
Him tellin' me tales of the sea
with waves like mountains climbing to the sky
and great steel ships longer than the river is wide
thrown about like toys. "I have to pee Grampa."
He said,
"Pee in the river boy
and watch it travel with the flow."
I asked him where the river goes.
"The river, Lad? It flows all the way to forever.
Then someday, like me, it will reach Fiddler's Green."
"Where's that place, Fiddler's Green?"
"Well, Dicky, Fiddler's Green is the place
where the souls of sailors go."
"Is it a nice place?"
"It's a grand place, with many a lass,
and many a glass and never a stormy sea."
The corner bar beckoned us.
We slipped into a booth. He sat across from me
and slid the full nickel glass towards me
and I drank deep of the cool brew.
We were soon joined by other big brawny Irishmen.
They talked of the Old Country, and life's ebb and flow.
Wide eyed and open-minded I listened.
I especially remember the Sullivan Brothers,
they had been professional rasslers.
On the side they hauled sand and gravel.
They had horse drawn steel wagons.
The wheels were also steel
and a big steel handle brake on the side
welded to a ratchet, to lock up the wheels.
They had cauliflower ears, pug noses,
and lots of scar tissue around their eyes.
Tall powerful men with big thick hands.

1

And I knew in my childish heart
I was one of them.
Though they were big and powerful
and could be mean, I was one of them.
As I look back over three score and some,
that cool brew on a hot summer day
when I was welcomed into the family of man
was the sweetest of them all.

QUEEN OF THE CHARLES

That Grampa of mine
convinced me I could do anything.
Yes, even build a boat all my own.
I scavenged the neighborhood.
I found some weathered junk wood,
a torn and rotten piece of canvas,
a pocket full of rusted bent nails
and I had the raw material
for building my first boat.
I set my imagination, my mind to the task.
It took what seemed a long time.
Maybe all of three days.
It was shaped like the letter 'A'.
I wanted a pointed bow to cut through the waves.
Because of the nature of the junk wood
there were many holes
where the river could flow in.
That's where the canvas would work
to cover those holes.
I had me a boat!
I called her 'Queen of the Charles'
after the Queen Mary which my Grampa
convinced me was a mighty ship.
I rounded up a couple of my pals
to help me carry the Queen to the river
for the promise of a crossing.
The launching of one's boat
is like giving birth to dreams.
It is a time of excitement, ecstasy,
joy, and party time.
The sun was warm and the river wide.
We put the Queen in the water
and for a minute or two
I knew the glory of a dream fulfilled.
Until the river filled my boat
making it disappear in the dark and the deep.

IN LONGFELLOW PARK
Cambridge, 1935

I got older and Grampa got slower.
By the age of seven I was mostly conscious.
We would sit for hours in Longfellow Park.
He would talk about the "Book of Life".
Expecting me to learn its secrets:
"It's not enough, Boy, to know the words;
you can't put the inner fire in words.
Nor can a man contain it in his heart ...
why, that would be like locking God in a book.
A book is only a book,
but the inner fire is the force behind creation.
Without it, you're nothing more
than dumb cattle, cannon fodder;
the dross and snuff of humankind.
Though someone has to bring in the harvest,
cook and clean.
I've walloped many a pot in my time.
I deeply appreciate a good galley utility man.
One that can do it with a song in his heart.
There's many a sad soul lives a life
of toil, drudgery, and despair;
lucky to get an hour or two,
now an' agin, to find a little joy in life.
Like the poet said, 'My life
is cold, and dark, and dreary ...'
There are some work to live
and nothing more.
'Tis a far better thing to work
for the sheer love of the work ...
and give an honest day's work
for an honest day's pay.
A working man must be able to afford the essentials;
A pint of Guinness on a Sunday mornin',
An egg now an' agin with his mornin' toast.
Ah ... 'tis a good life, if you have the heart for it.
Dicky, my boy,
of all the ships I've sailed

4

from backwater tropical ports
to the cold Arctic night,
ah, the questions I've asked,
and the places I've looked ...
then one day, after I had given up,
I found it, Boy. I found my Kingdom ..."
He paused. I waited.
Finally I asked,
"Where'd you find it Grampa,
the Kingdom, where?"
"Don't expect me to tell you that.
It might dampen the fire
that drives the quest.
Stoke it, lad, stoke it.
Breathe deep. Let yer heart glow.
You'll need all you've got
to ride out the gales and storms.
It's done with heart, boy,
Aye, lad, plenty of heart
And if'n you've a smile in yer heart
You'll come out laughing with joy,
For the thrill of it all."

THE CALL

I stood on a shore of solid rock
and felt the sea rolling in big and slow,
standing up and reaching for the sky,
breaking, spreading her foam in the air,
slapping and splashing the rocks, hard,
like thunder, the earth trembled.
She smelled strong and fertile from raking her depths,
like a woman giving birth when it's everything that is.
There was no horizon, only fog,
and above the fog, the summer sun.
I felt her beauty, heard her promise,
and the sound and the smell of the sea
possessed me like my mother,
floating in the saline sack of her womb,
the fruit of friendly thighs.

DREAMS

Dreams, warmed by the heart,
can drive a man.
They can drive him to where there is no time,
a place where he plays all day
riding waves in Fiddler's Green.
When a man sets sail on the winds of dreams
he believes in a God who resides in his imagination
and nothing is impossible or beyond his reach;
without beginning and without end.
In the imagination there is magic and miracles,
ideas and laughter.
My imagination can reach down into dark despair
cutting the darkness with its light,
and the smoldering love that sighs in my soul
can reach again, and again for the wave crest.
My heart beats in rhythm to the pounding of the surf,
drawing my soul as the moon draws the tide,
where beautiful flowers emit their scent
spreading their petals with welcoming
that they may bear fruit
and know the regeneration of the flesh
that eases the pain of living and decay.
I sigh, satisfied with life's cycle,
and my mind rejoices in the spirit.

POETRY, BUT WHY

Poetry can be like soul food
able to put a smile in one's heart,
sometimes a smile with a tear of joy,
at other times a 'right-on' in the mind,
if it has that universality of oneness.
In those times when all hope is lost
when the doldrums envelop one's mind
a poem, like a loving smile,
can lighten the soul and one can overcome.
A poem can be a warm and tender body
or a hot cup of coffee and a friend.
It can open the door for thinking things over,
it can stoke the embers of your heart
and you can once more feel the heat
of a young lover in days long ago.
A poem can show you the stupidity
and the horrors of War.
A poem can awaken your humanity.
A poem can be a cool drink of water
when you wander in dry places
seeking the warmth of love
and finding only fear of love.
A poem can open your heart and mind
and you can experience and know, maybe:
In each of us is all of us.
I knew poetry was for me
when I first read:
"The world is so full of a number of things
I'm sure we should all be as happy as Kings."
Poetry has given me lessons in loving.
It has given me the courage
to pursue the height and depths of love,
love's ecstasy, its bliss,
its Godliness
and its immortality.
Poetry has stoked my imagination
to live a dream and know a place

where I have conquered time and space
and Love is King of Kings
as I surf the exit of the Black Hole;
like a neutrino, part of everything that is.
Poetry can cut through verbosity
and say it like it is.
A narrative poem can say
what it wants to say in a few pages;
a novel might take five or six hundred.
When I've broken a bone
I go to a doctor.
When my heart has been broken
I go to a poet.
Some people pray to a sky god
for help, or to fulfill dreams.
I pull a poem from my mind
and listen with my heart.

LEAVING HOME

I've traveled by thumb, air, sea and land,
going away from a place called 'home'.
Home was a hard time kind of place;
there wasn't much time for being a kid
and doing the things kids get off on.
There was no time for talking about things,
things you needed to know to make a life,
like what makes the wind blow, why
and where does the sun go at night.
After Mom died I was just another motherless pup.
I had a job and I went to school.
From the age of nine it was expected I earn my keep;
an experience I've shared with most of the world;
an experience that leads to the acceptance of,
"We are One."
Perhaps that's why I feel at home
no matter where in the world I am.
If school interfered with the job
then school would have to yield to the job.
Changes came fast and furious
with a World War going on across the ocean.
I'd always be reading the papers in those days,
perhaps that came from an inner knowing
that knowledge is strength, wealth and freedom.
One day in the classified, I read:
"Seamen wanted. No experience necessary.
Will train. Must be sixteen years old."
So I shipped out with other sixteen year-olds
in a Liberty ship loaded down to its gunnels
with five inch artillery shells.
We spent Christmas of 44 in Marseilles
with the Luftwaffe dropping bombs.
My seventeenth birthday I spent in Liverpool
with an English honey and a pint of half and half.
Best thing I ever did was to leave home.

SHIPPING OUT

A steel Liberty ship low in the water,
heavy with bombs for killing the enemy.
Running down a following sea, shipping it green,
she quivers clean down to her keel.
I can feel her steel straining in my gut.
and in my mind's eye I see
raiders lurking in the dark and the deep
to send us all to kingdom come.
Then out of the War Zone,
south past the Tropic of Cancer,
the sun coming up like God creating light.
A dark sea comes alive with color dancing in a mirror.
Picking up a pilot to guide us
down a muddy river,
the air thick with the fertile smell of the tropics.
At the dilapidated wooden dock
large burlap sacks of raw sugar
waited for us to stow aboard.
Puerto Tarrafa had its dock and nothing more.
Nuevites was only a mile down the road and had cantinas,
and there Latin ladies working for the Yankee dollar
took advantage of my sweet sixteen innocence
as they sexually harassed me
until Carmelita, a young beauty,
a few months older than me
pulled me aside and pinned me against the wall
with her full breast and warm undulating stomach ...
And it came to pass in that time and place,
beyond a doubt,
that Carmelita had awakened in me
the joy of creation with a taste of Ecstasy.
She wanted me to jump ship and be her man.
She spoke from her heart
but I laughed.
She walked away from me angry.
But today, miles and years away,

when the skies are gray
and the drizzle cold and dreary,
I wonder what a life I might have made
back there in Cuba so far away.
Perhaps my spirit would have glowed bright
as I stood and fought with my brother, Che,
for the love and dignity of humankind.
Together, arm in arm, soul brothers,
to drive the evil murderous Batista
from the backs of the peasants.
There is poetry in a life like that.
Regardless, I have done something.
I spoke out against the cockroach,
head of the Federal Secret Police.
I vomited at the pile of doo doo
who became president and spent tomorrow
in an arms race for the benefit of his
military/industrial sponsors.
I criticize myself, but what have you done?

POINT OF REFERENCE

Once there was a time
when I only knew three forms of matter,
but none of them really mattered,
when I wandered aimless with the stars
and came back to look inside my heart
and find an all encompassing love,
born of a lighting rod from God
that took the form of a teenage girl
and gave me a glimpse of the Almighty's power.
I let go of mind and surrendered
to the totality of my experience.
But your daddy told you I was after
only one thing.
We both knew he was talking about 'down there'.

Without heart and love in a box
I went off in reckless abandon
to experience this world and 'doing it'.
With my heart on hold I was ever true to you.
Then there came a day here and now,
when those regrets and grievances of all my life
dissolved in the light of forgiveness
and I learned to love ... and how sweet it is
without the pain of yesterday's regrets.

My love for you
gave me the experience of love's bliss.
This point of reference for love's bliss
was like the holy grail, immortality,
but I had only a glance
in a moment beyond time and space.
Yet that moment was enough.

THE NORTHERN SEAS
Isle of Wight, 1966

When you've sailed the Northern seas
and seen what I have seen,
you don't go back to the girl at home
with your seabag all unpacked.
For the bitter storms of winter come
with the wild wind passing through,
and you look upon the skies at night
and wonder what it's like,
for your mates out there, where heaven's rare
and hell's a peaceful sight.
The girl at home don't mean a damn
when the wild wind's passing through,
for you'll feel your life's a bottle spent
unless you're there where you belong
with tired mates in an all-night fight
where sleep's a wide-eyed dream.
And you'll take your pick when they meet the ship
of a London tart who's true
for a pint of mild and a bag of chips
and every quid you've earned
from a hellish trip
where the wild wind howled,
"Fool, it's Davy Jones for you!"

GUIDO
Ibiza, September 1967

I met him in the fall of the year on the island of Ibiza
living aboard his boat the BlackViking,
a retired thirty foot day racer built in Sweden.
A previous owner had put a cabin on it
just high enough to sit in bending over.
Guido bought it, with its worn out sails,
for a cruising home afloat.
By trade he was a merchant seaman radio operator,
but by hair style and a far away look in his eye
he looked like Lord Byron in search of the Goddess.
When he needed money he'd ship out
but much preferred the freedom of uncharted seas
where a sailor might cruise to Fiddler's Green.
The young cruising sailor is a rare
and mysterious breed of man
driven by the quiet certainty of wide awake dreams.
In the summer he met a young English girl;
she was visiting Ibiza on a holiday.
When school called her back to Falmouth
the Black Viking was Guido's way to follow her.
Guided by a Higher Power that possessed his heart,
he had no other choice.
It was late in October, that time of year
when the violent storms of winter first begin
and come roaring across the forties of the cold Atlantic.
He readied the Black Viking for Falmouth
with tender care and a lover's prayer.
She sat low in the water with little freeboard.
He could lean over the side and wash his hands.
From clew to tack the old main was worn,
he used a three foot reef to hold it on.
He had no motor if the wind should rage
and tear his rotten main to rags,
but he had a long oak oar to see him through.

For part of the voyage he had a carefree crew,
amateur lads, in ignorant folly, their first time out,
when nothing is impossible and everyday is new.
The two whites would get off in Gibraltar.
The African American, used to abuse,
had nothing to lose but the clothes on his back;
he'd sail all the way, or so he thought.
Guido shared his boat, his rice and his beans,
and any fish caught would be a welcome feast.
He sailed away on a late October day.
I sailed alongside for a short way
and furled my sails to watch him fade
beyond the line where sea meets sky.
Then one day, when a week had gone by,
I was sitting in the cockpit enjoying the sun,
when down the dock a young woman walked
with all the splendor of womanhood;
her loveliness crowned in a wealth of golden brown hair
radiating a presence to be all she was meant to be.
The lovely flowers of spring, of fertility,
delicate warmth glowed about her.
Yet in that delicate, warmth and softness
I knew in my heart here was a woman
whose look could be a thunderbolt
that would spoil a man for all others.
In front of my boat she looked at me and held my eyes,
"Do you know Guido's boat, the Black Viking?"
"Yes, he left about a week ago."
As if a chill wind swept away the warm sun she shivered.
"O, that's too bad. I wanted to go with him."
She turned and walked back down the dock
but the ethereal vibrant quality had changed,
as if her heart had gone someplace else.
I jumped to the dock and shouted after her, "Wait!"
She turned, "Yes?"
"He planned on stopping in Gibraltar.
If you really want to sail with him

catch a bus to Gibraltar.
You might even get there before him."
Spirit and heart returned to her. She thanked me.
In another week I sailed for the island of Malta
where I'd planned to spend the winter
obeying my Muse, giving me work
that was piling up
and spoiling me for all else.
In December I read in an English newspaper
that the Black Viking was long overdue in Falmouth.
Overdue? That violent hungry Bay of Biscay
had swallowed Guido and his boat.
The sailor in me knew it was true.
But the poet in me saw a different reality:
When there is love, there is no fear of death
and of the earthly powers of a Poseidon, or Zeus,
for when two hearts are committed in love
they abide forever in the heart of the God of Gods.
And not all the false gods of this world
can ever change a part of that.
Rather than see Guido and his beloved entwined,
rotting in the muck at the bottom of the Bay of Biscay,
I see them extending love,
and creating beauty in Paradise.

SOCRATES TELLS A STORY

In the beginning man was as God,
complete in and of himself,
for he had been created
in the image and likeness of God.
Man made an ego and became ambitious.
He wanted to be more powerful than God.
When God saw man's foolishness
God decided to teach man a lesson.
God divided him into negative and positive,
into Yin and Yang, into male and female,
then scattered the parts about the earth
so that man and woman
might never again know Paradise
until they found their other half.

FOG AND SUN IN THE CHANNEL

Sailing off the Saltee Islands single-handed in fog
when the fog is thick as pudding;
is coma any different?
Then night comes down
and all is blackness
and you begin to see things,
things bigger than life,
coming at you in the fog like light,
telling you things, not with words
but putting them in your mind
and you give thanks for your oil skins
and your Irish Knit in the wet chill
of the grave.
Sailing off the same Saltee Islands
with an Irish barrister and his eighteen year-old daughter
whose hero was Che Guevara.
The barrister had as much Kipling
committed to memory as me
and we entertained each other
with poetry and Bushmills,
while the lovely daughter prepared the lobster
from a lobsterman working around the Saltees.
There were white clouds moving fast,
there was the warmth of the sun,
the wind filled the shoulder of our sails.
I wanted nothing more.

SEA STORY

I sailed on past the Goodwin Sands
half a day free of confining land,
a free-lance sailor, a carefree rover,
I sailed on through the Straits of Dover
to meet the Channel boiling over
in big black water without a sky
where the wind sang me his song,
"I Spit in Your Eye."
Blown through the night
beyond the Dungeness Light
with the phosphorous fire
that burns on the crest
when the wind screams his ire
and pounds on his chest.
My son asleep in his berth below-
nine years young-
would he never grow old?
My flesh gone numb
and my soul gone cold,
I cursed the salt of the sea in my eyes
while the wallowing wind
breathed a victory sigh,
as he took a pause in the middle of the sky
and I prayed to God he would wither and die.
By all God's angels
and all God's might
I saw on that dark and stormy night
the skeletal worried wistful lives
of a hundred ghostly English Lymes
infinitely stroking at their oars,
to eternity, a vanishing door.
They stared at me when I stared at them
and they spoke in a voice mired with kelp for phlegm,
"YOU, YOU FOOL,
WHAT ARE YOU DOING HERE?
US, WE HAD TO BE HERE,

BUT YOU WHY?"
I turned my head and closed my eyes
as they left me there to wonder why
in the dark by and by
while the wind grew tired,
curled up and died.
But he left in his calm a sorcerer's balm
that gave no peace in the here and now.
With my dreams of tomorrow I sailed on west
seeking a place to feast and rest,
pursuing a hiding peaceful sun
full four long years and then some,
'til a wind whipped longing
built for me a better ship,
born to the sea with a forestay sprit.
And the wide world opened to call her down
for fun and frolic and a merry-go-round.
I faced the sea with a confident show
and sailed the break on the tidal flow
to meet the wind in half a gale.
He soon defied my scrawny dreams
as he urged me on with a madman's screams,
full high his gale and on I sailed
drinking my fill of his devil's ale.
His anger grew and turned me around
to batter and pound.
He took hold of my bow
to twist me and toss me and take me in tow.
And before the day had quite begun,
as I looked for the light from the morning sun,
he showed me tomorrow
where fools try to borrow
lifeless and hollow
no joy and no sorrow.
And the voice of those ghostly kelp-covered Lymes
came back to this night when the wind was unkind,

21

to ask me,
"WHY DO YOU LIVE
AND WHY DO YOU DIE?"
Then out of the wind and the foam of the sea
I saw a goddess on my starboard lee.
She had skin and bones and a golden glow.
I smiled at her and she smiled at me
with a love that said we were born to be
in this moment now and for eternity.
I heard with my heart, I heard her sigh.
I saw with my soul, I saw her cry,
her heart filled with giving God's reason why
and silence forever Death's victory lie.

SHIPWRECK

1.

The nature of a Creator is to create.
Creation is an ongoing process like the Universe itself;
like evolution is an ongoing process
just like creation. Though I can't tell the difference.
To me, it's all mind and
I came to know I was as mighty as my mind ...
and nestled in my mind
the powers of creation wait. Patiently they wait.
Bombarded by nos, can'ts, laws and obstacles.
But one day the stuff of dreams,
the inner fire
permeated the totality that is me
and all doubt vanished.
When that ethereal quality became solid matter
and I was able to lean against it and not fall.
Seeing what I had formed with mind,
blood and sweat surprised me
and I was in awe of my own power.
That was the beginning of the manifestation
of Fiddler's Green.
With single mindedness of purpose,
possessiveness of spirit,
I had toiled every waking and free moment
on a boat that would take me to the wave crest,
to a place where only love and beauty are real.
Sick to the core with the insanity of this world
I wanted none of its madness.
I determined to leave it all behind and fly
like a dream in flight with the tropical trades
to a place where love is all-encompassing.

2.

This sweet sea-chariot of mine
would carry me with the winds to beyond,
where there are no national boundaries,
and the laws of men and nations don't exist.
She would be an autonomous world
with me as the Captain calling the shots
and malice towards none.
The warmth and tenderness of womankind
was always welcome aboard
as was the camaraderie of men
with laughter in their heart
filling the night and riding a smiling breeze.
There would be drink aboard
with rum for the doldrums
and single malt from the glens of Scotland
to purge my heart of yesterday's regrets
and free my heart of tomorrow's unknowns.
The table would overflow with fresh shrimp
from the Gulf of Tehuantepec,
lobster from the waters off Todos Santos
and abalone from Turtle Bay.
There would be Dorado as I sailed west,
or other endless treasures I might dream of.
And why not?
I had dreamt of Fiddler's Green
and she became real and was beautiful to behold.

3.

She was launched on November the 30th in 72.
As she slid down the launching ramp,
and floated on her own,
all my yesterdays drifted away.
This was to be a new beginning
on a course laid out for Fiddler's Green.
There were five double berths
and a stormberth in the wheelhouse for me
when the wind and sea were misbehaving.
Her ketch rig could carry
two thousand square feet of working sail.
A Perkins Diesel in the engine compartment
and enough fuel if the wind should fail
to motor half way to Maui.
She had a refrigerator in the galley,
two toilets and a shower.
Expensive chrome winches and a ship-to-shore dingy.
Twenty-two feet wide
and forty-nine feet to the tip of her bowsprit.
Capable of carrying her working sails in a gale.
My self assurance in her size and safety
faded before dawn one morning
in a storm off the Farallons,
when the wind and driving sea blew into my mind
the words of an Aran Islander
when asked, if they be afraid of the sea?
"Them that don't be afraid of the sea
goes to sea when they oughten ta
and they git drownd-ed.
But here, we do be afraid of the sea
and only git drownd-ed now and agin."

4.

Not having made the transition
from the dedicated focus of boat-builder
to being-where-you-are;
my dream driven mind ran before the wind
to nine degrees north latitude
and eighty-four degrees west longitude
and a few degrees in between
to where the trade winds in the deep tropics prevail.
I had no partner to help run the boat.
Being skipper and first mate was more than a chore;
It was a shoddy way to spend my days.
With plenty of berths there were plenty of takers
and discernment in me was a lesson to learn.
O, but I soon tired
of picking up towels, bathing suits, dirty socks.
Shopping for food, cooking food, washing up.
Those able to take responsibility
for themselves and garbage were few.
The men generally needed mothers, or wives,
maybe a servant to clean up and pick up after them,
driving me to play the role of a Wolf Larson.
The women were slightly better
but with my time and mind
wholly possessed by Fiddler's Green
I found little time for love's amenities;
and none became my partner.
Seasick people were useless.
Homesick people would pine and then fly away.
Some were great while they lasted.

It was in Puerto Vallarta that I wrote:

'ODE TO A ONE NIGHT STAND'

I listened to you sing your hard rock
all the way back to the stone age,
a lovely piece of meat, New York cut,
and you didn't give a damn about my soul.
Though the UFOs were shot down by IUDs
on their way to the automatic society,
when your solid state went dry for want of juice,
and fertility fused neither you nor I.
Though god knows how I tried
to believe in color TV and the FCC
but all I saw were shades of gray
on the unemployment screen.
It was somewhere near your nylon cheeks,
essence of acetone,
that I found the Teflon-coated valley
smothered in promises, a petroleum by-product
that couldn't breed mildew in the dark,
open to the general public
for artificial treats, believe in me
Howard Johnson is down the street
eager to please the family of man.
I tried to get past the chemical overkill
looking for life,
but you can't scratch Teflon
with a poet's knife.
If only I had rented a TV for the night
I could have watched my country die
trying to grow synthetic people with artificial cries
and preserved a dream or two
til my heart found someone more real than you.

5.

Take a pause along with me
from bodies in search of ecstasy
to where late spring and early summer merge
to form a perfect day
and all is right in the universe.
I loved Mexico. I still do.
The mountains, and snaking the Durango Pass,
the beaches, and settling into a palapa,
the palm trees joining in chorus with the sea breeze.
The Central Mercado with its sounds,
its colors and smells ...
the smiling faces and shinning eyes
of its young girls dancing into womanhood.
The mothers enjoying and cuddling their young,
the open smiling faces of their children.
The strength, the camaraderie, the commitment
of the young men as they struggle and fight
their way north to sweat and toil
in the factories and fields of the gringos ...
to be ripped off by the coyotes and the grower,
deported by the INS ... but not defeated.
Coming back time and time and time after time.
To enjoy a country, a people, a person, is like love,
it feels very good in the area of the heart.

6.

In San Jose, Guatemala, I picked up a mooring
while Poseidon, breathing a rhythmic deep sigh
tossed up giant swells, slow, strong and high.
That gave Fiddler's Green and her crew a restless stay.
A gold-braided general, a gold-braided admiral,
a gold-braided captain of the port,
all men of very great self importance,
came aboard with flushed faces and fat bellies
that spoke loudly of their wealth and affluence.
They were nervous and projected fear
that I might be carrying guns for the peasants
who wanted just a little piece of what they had.
Was I their enemy they wondered?
Supporting the communists in their midst?
In reality they knew as much about communism
as they knew about the proverbial bogeyman.
Or perhaps I was like their patron, Kissinger,
their supporter who knew the Indians
and peasants to be dirty ignorant animals?...
who could only understand
the gun, brutality and death?
I had a four-liter jug of Mexican rum
and poured them all a few fingers.
We drank to United Fruit
and continued military support;
but in my heart I prayed
they would slide to hell
on the blood of the innocents they slaughtered.
In the streets and along the beach
I saw the fruits of America's foreign policy
in the hungry swollen bellies of babies,
in their big pitiful pleading eyes.
I felt a wretchedness in my heart
for their pain.
I saw a young mother all in black, walking proud
behind her murdered husband's coffin,
a human rights activist,
who felt the pain of the oppressed and hungry,

stood up, spoke out, was counted,
then murdered by the Kill Squads.
A young man who spoke good English
saw me with his third eye and said,
"Our people suffer. They are hungry.
It would be good to see something done.
You live in a free country. You vote.
Can you not do something?
The military, you give them much money.
They are very strong, they kill many people.
Why do you do this?"
I told him,
"We have many ignorant assholes
in high political office.
They are there because ignorant voters
are bought and sold with TV ads."
In Acajutla, El Salvador,
the guard patrolled the waterfront
and the American-trained and-financed
Kill Squads were the best dollars could buy.
They could kill Bishops and Jesuits alike,
rape and kill nuns with impunity.
"Love," they sneered,
"We can hire peasants to kill peasants.
Brother to kill brother."

7.

In Puntarenas, Costa Rica, I rested for awhile,
many miles from all my yesterdays of searching;
driven by a restless wind that knew no peace.
I found in the Golfo de Nicoya, a bit of Utopia.
The fishing was easy, almost jumping aboard,
and the ladies welcomed the strokes
from a seagoing man.
But I had sailed Fiddler's Green hard
and she needed work.
The clew on her working jib had torn out
and three times been sewn back.
The radio direction finder
was transformed into useless junk.
The refrigerator gave up its cooling
and the engine's heat exchanger followed
when it sucked up sand from the bottom
of the lagoon in Bara Navidad.
I was learning the vulnerability of high-tech,
the possessiveness of possessions.
The bigger the boat, the bigger the job.
The more equipment aboard, the more to breakdown.
My dream boat had become
a possessive pain in the ass.
I determined to take her to San Diego and sell her,
and the next time I set out to sea
would be in a smaller boat ...
just me and a partner working as one.
The perfect crew for the cruising life.

8.

I headed north against the wind and the sea,
close hauled under gray skies,
with an occasional day of surfing the crests
and running down a following sea at flank speed.
After an exhilarating beat with the sea in a scud
I arrived in Mazatlan and my unpaid crew deserted
leaving me alone to prepare
for the beat up Baja and home.
On a sport fishing dock in the inner harbor
lived and worked, Eddie. Eighteen years old, maybe.
He was about five feet two inches tall
and about one hundred and twenty pounds.
He was being paid fifteen dollars a month
to do pick-up and clean-up;
his berth was under the awning on a cement patio, sans bedding.
In broken Spanish and sign language
I made it known I needed a sailor.
His eyes opened wide,
he straightened his back, lifted his chest
and vowed with an oath:
"Me, me you man."
He quit his job and moved aboard,
to be my first mate working for room and board.
A change of clothes and a child's guitar
he brought to sustain him crossing the bar.
Eddie was a gift committed to me,
and with my man Friday I'd head back to sea.
Like soul brothers we were, or father and son,
with love and respect and working as one.
We shared in the work and we shared in the food
and the laughter and joy of being alive.
Up the river we beached the boat on an island
made of brush and mud that would often flood.
We crawled on our bellies rolling in muck
scraping, scrubbing and painting her bottom
with never a thought for the leaches that suck.

9.

To the outer harbor, washed and ready,
the paper work pending on bureaucratic formality,
we waited and Eddie played his small guitar
while I laid back, a peaceful skipper,
enjoying the moment and my day in the sun.
I met a gringa woman at a party one night
among twenty expatriates drunk out of sight.
She told me she was a prisoner in need
of a helping hand to escape the man
who had shackled her to him for pleasure and sin.
I left the house and she followed me out
and begged me to take her to my home afloat.
To deny a lady in distress
would destroy my heart and shatter my honor.
I took her aboard and she wanted to score.
She drank all my rum and wanted more.
Then she sent for her daughter
to help her decide on a place to go
where she might grow young, and once more know
there is a yesterday she might borrow
and never, never have to face tomorrow.
Her daughter arrived, sweet and tender,
full of bosom that spoke, "Eighteen and ripe."
She told me her mom was jealous of her
for being more woman with juices to spare.
Eager to show me and hungry to prove
in the juices that flowed a fire that glowed.
Her soft murmuring cries took hold of my hand
and plied to explore near her plump rounded thighs
her Mound of Venus and the promised prize.
And I remember the night on Fiddler's Green
with a lovely young lass on the wheelhouse floor
doing the things men and women adore.
We lifted anchor and hoisted sail

with mom and daughter, and Eddie and me.
I set the course for homeward bound,
seasick all, but Eddie and me.
I turned around and took them to town
And waited again to clear the port.

10

It was dusk one evening in early September,
fog laid over the harbor, I clearly remember.
We had just finished dinner and settled to smoke,
when across the water and down the hatch came a shout,
we went on deck and looked about
through the fog and mist for a human voice.
The sky was blue but the fog was low,
the only shore was a hazy glow.
Then through the fog all wrapped in mist
a derelict skiff came drifting, sculling by.
An old hatless Mexican with a toothless grin
one hand working the skull, the other waving, "Hola, Hola."
On the single seat sat two young women.
They smiled with a smile open and gay,
a blond and brunette they made a lovely bouquet.
With steady brown eyes the brunette looked at me,
and with a confident voice:
"Hi, we heard you were going to California
and might want somebody to help crew?"
Beauty in the sky or beauty in the eye
gripped my heart shoving reason aside.
I invited them aboard to discuss the matter
where we engaged in very friendly chatter.
Sofia, the brunette, was the older of two.
Julie, the blond, had eyes a deep blue;
And a warmth that said, "I love to screw."
Eddie quite speechless, the smallest of all
was bewildered in awe and culturally shocked.
I hadn't been looking for a crew,
confident Eddie and I could go it alone.
The ladies, I soon found out
didn't know a jib from a jibe,
and had no interest in learning.
Somewhere in the primordial ooze of my being
I knew that to deny these young women
would be a sin against creation.
Poseidon, himself, might rise from the depths

and swallow me, Fiddler's Green and all,
in a vortex of infinity.
Into the cosmos that was Fiddler's Green
they brought beauty, a vitality that springs from health,
physical strength and a love of life,
with confidence and trust in themselves.
Sofia was nineteen. Julie was eighteen.
While Eddie and I worked on Fiddler's Green
Sofia and Julie would lie topless on the cabin top,
bikini underpants hiding not the least of the promise.
The Creator did Herself proud with those beauties.
Their presence nurtured my soul.
When the sun became too hot,
they would dive overboard in a smooth arc,
hardly a splash, swim and frolic,
jump up in the water, grab the bowsprit,
swing aboard with laughter and graceful ease.
They showered in the cockpit with the portable shower
refusing the amenities of a curtain
that might hide their beauty.
Perfect works of art. Water nymphs.
One bronze and one a translucent marble.
Their bodies and beauty needed no touching up,
and I enjoyed their beauty as I enjoy a blooming rose.
Sofia had an unblemished coffee colored skin.
There were no lines between tan and white;
she was the same in every crack and crevice.
Her firm young breasts perfect in size and shape.
Julie looked like Botticelli's Venus.
All about her she had a fine golden down
that reflected the sun in a bright aura.
Her hair cascaded naturally in golden silk like waves
and her Mound of Venus
had the same full richness and color.
They showered with an unselfconscious confidence
that killed any lecherous remarks
even before such remarks could be born.
They had the kind of beauty
man has elevated to pedestals
since he first found his soul.

They would please the soul of a Michelangelo
and any poet or sailor with a soul.
There was nothing bimbo about them
nor were they crotch-grabbing Madonnas,
flaunting and teasing with their charms.
They were proud free women loving themselves,
enjoying life and living.

11

Julie loved to snuggle and be snuggled.
She would come to my berth in the still of night
and we shared the peace and warmth of love.
Whether Poseidon's daughter, or a siren from the sea
her beauty was a jewel of great worth.
wholly loving and lovable.
Her kisses were warm and sweet
like the seawater I breathed before I breathed air
in that warm sac of my gestation.
Those mysterious beauties that entered my life
through a foggy mist to complete my dream
were flesh, bone, blood and heart
radiating the glory of womankind ...
they celebrated their independence and freedom in being
like a celestial song sung to the sounds of the sea.
Eddie in shock would lie for hours on his bunk,
his eyes open, looking at nothing, every nerve awake,
every heartbeat listening, wondering in wonderland.
The macho role models of his childhood deserted him.
Sofia and Julie treated him with the affection
of a younger brother needing disciplinary sustenance.

12.

We left Mazatlan in the middle of September.
In total calm the Sea of Cortez reflected the sky.
At the end of the first day, heading due west,
the compass pointed to the setting sun on the horizon,
like a door of light into another world.
Time stood still.
The beauty and majesty of the moment silenced us.
Slowly the earth rolled on and night unfolded into
a light show of stars and an endless and perfect universe
that filled our hearts with a song of praise.
In the wheelhouse I held the wheel steady on course;
Julie came to me and leaned against me.
The closeness of her warmth pleased me.
I put an arm around her.
She laid her head on my chest.
As it was in the beginning, man and woman together,
given the earth and everything in it.
I experienced being me without desire,
free at last of unfulfilled dreams.
That day and night I realized
a finer firmament of the Fiddler's Green dream.
In the still of night I wrote Julie a poem:

Julie, I sing of your beauty.
A song of praise and adoration.
The nearness of your warm presence
fills me to overflowing with joy
and I can feel the ecstasy of creation
burning with the inner fire of my heart.
I can compare thee to nothing I have known
for thou art a paradigm shift in my consciousness,
a quantum leap in what is beauty.
So complete in and of yourself
of all that womankind has been to man ...
from the birthing bed to the death bed.
May your loins bring forth

strong men and women, tempered in truth,
true to their higher self unto death.
May the bloom of your ripe fruit-bearing beauty
shine for all eternity for men to adore.

13.

We made stops at Cabo San Lucas and Magadelena Bay,
and up the coast of Baja sailing close-hauled
Fiddle's Green danced on the sea
galloping through the troughs and racing the crests.
North by northwest we crawled into colder seas
and the skies sagged low with a leaden gray.
With the Tropic of Cancer far behind
and slightly inclined to turn her around
a bit of truth came back to my mind;
and truth is an ever constant fact,
and that only constant is trust in change.
On the 30th of September, I remember, I remember ...
thirty miles south of Ensenada,
at dusk I pointed her bow due west
to clear all the headlands we'd pass in the night.
By midnight I'd pick up the lights off Todos Santos,
if they were working, but either way,
we should pass safely outside
and the following day we would be in San Diego
where Fiddler's Green would be sold.

14.

We were motor-sailing close-hauled,
with the wheel secured slightly to port.
She was well-balanced enough to steer herself.
Her designer had assured me
I needed no electronic auto pilot;
it might fail when most needed.
As a skipper I always tried to give twice to the ship
what I expected from the crew.
They were unpaid. Sailing for fun.
Eddie was tired, worn to the core.
He had been up most of the previous night with me
trying to resuscitate the engine's heat exchanger.
I wanted him rested for the early morning hours.
And me, my neurotransmitters had shut down.
A total fatigue staggered and overwhelmed me.
I was sure it would subside
if only I could lie down for an hour.
I asked Julie if she'd take the watch for that hour.
She came into the wheelhouse with a blanket,
sat in the pilot chair and wrapped herself up.
I gave her instructions.
"Our course is 292 degrees, West Northwest.
If the compass should vary
from its present position wake me.
Keep an eye out for lights ... any light,
and wake me if you see anything.
It is now seven-thirty
but wake me no later than eight-thirty."
I laid down in the pilot berth,
an arm's length away from her.
Within seconds I was sound asleep.
A very deep, deep sleep of total fatigue.
Then minutes later Julie was asleep.
We slept in peace while Fiddler's Green sailed on.

15.

While we slept a rogue wave altered our course
ninety degrees to starboard.
On a broad reach my home afloat sailed smoothly
towards the rocks of Punta San Jose.
At ten-thirty, 2230 hours, while deep in my sleep
I felt the bottom of Fiddler's Green touch rock.
My sleep ended.
I awoke to a world that was a nightmare.
The wheel was in my hand in a heartbeat.
On the port side was a solid wall of black cliff,
to starboard ... breaking seas.
The night was black and the only light in the sky
was the small masthead light of Fiddler's Green
waving crazily against an empty night sky.
The breaking sea burnt its phosphorescent fire
lighting up my boat and the rocks that imprisoned us.
I hit the throttle to full ahead
and turned the wheel hard to starboard.
Nothing but the continued crunching of the rocks,
smashing and tearing us.
I tried reversing.
I could now see the rocks in her belly
tearing out her guts,
tearing my treasure into slivers.
Within minutes the seas were sloshing about
in the main cabin.

16.

We were living the fury of shipwreck
while some great monster from the deep
using big sharp rocks for teeth
crunched and munched all that we were
in an unknown desolate dark place
where violence reigned supreme.
The sails slapped uselessly like a beating whip,
adding to the violent disharmony of the breaking seas ...
the tearing and pounding of my boat ...
the putt-putt of the diesel engine so out of place
yet not quite drowned in sea water ...
though it soon sputtered and died.
Fiddler's Green was dying and I was helpless.
A fair wind would never again fill her sails.
Julie clung to me speechless and frightened ...
Eddie wiping deep sleep from his eyes soon joined us ...
Sofia arrived in the wheelhouse within seconds,
she asked, "What happened?"
The moment of truth blazed in every cell of my being
as the full fury of Death raged against us.
I told them all:
"We are being destroyed! You girls stay here. Sit on the bunk.
Eddie, get another flashlight,
and give me a hand getting the sails down."
Sofia and Julie were frightened but didn't panic.
Sofia asked, "We want to help. What can we do?"
To tell them, "Prepare to die,"
would that be wise?
I told them, "Get the life jackets out
from under the cockpit seats
and get some clothes and blankets for yourselves."

17.

In my mind my thoughts were afire,
Let Death rant and rave doing its thing.
I will not go humbly into its jaws.
With all my heart I deny Death and its totality.
So long as I breathe I deny him my soul.
If my time has come to merge with the everlasting
then I will do so with a will.

18.

Eddie stayed close by my side reading my mind,
open and receptive to my every thought.
Together we crawled to the mainmast
while the pounding surf lifted us in the air
and slammed us back down to the deck.
Crawling and clawing we reached the mainmast
and four hands working as one secured the sails.
We crawled back to the cockpit.
I leaned over the port side, the lee side,
shined my light into the blackness,
into the black teeth and the cascading surf.
I was lifted and jolted and slammed,
my flashlight flew from my hand
and continued to glow deep in its throat,
caught in a crevice of monster sharp molars
two fathoms deep.
Death seemed to sneer and gloat at me
like some butcher ready to devour me
with his knife like teeth.

19.

I did not know where we were.
It could not have been the islands of Todos Santos
for they did not have cliffs as black and high
as the high wall of blackness on our port side.
We must be somewhere on the mainland of Baja,
often a desolate part of the world,
more fit for a Tolkien novel than people.
Sofia and Julie clung together in the wheelhouse,
their eyes wide; they watched our every move.
Eddie was like my shadow moving with me
while I ground my teeth at the continuing demolition.
Seas sloshed about in the main cabin.
Debris floated between her ribs.
We were in the belly of the beast.
The broad beam of Fiddler's Green
prevented the beast from digesting us like fast food
until we were broken into bite size.
We, four souls, would be its desert.
In the seething turmoil of my mind
I found a moment of respite
and the hope of being regurgitated
from the belly of the beast.
I roared with laughter at Death's horror.
Holding on to a masthead stay,
standing on the roof of the cabin,
my body swaying with the lifting and the pounding
trying to look through the dark black night.
I wanted to reach into the bowels of death
and rip out its heart.
In my madness I shouted above the pounding surf,
"FUCK YOU, DEATH!"
The others looked at me
and with astonishment of heart
fear left them
and nervously they giggled.

20.

I knew Fiddler's Green.
I knew her every plank and board.
Her every nail and screw.
Her soul and her heart.
I had, with my mind and imagination,
with blood, with sweat and with muscle,
breathed life into her
and brought her into being.
I was her creator.
And now, in her final moments, I knew
she would sustain us through the night,
puppets on a string.
We had only Fiddler's Green ...
a Coast Guard in Mexico doesn't exist.

21.

It was Eddie who spotted the small light
coming down the cliff side
disappearing and seen again.
About fifteen feet above our level it stopped,
two hundred yards of lifetime away.
In the phosphorescent glow
we could see the dim outline of four men ...
in between the deafening sounds of the breaking surf
they shouted words carried away on the wind.
Time passes, even on death row, and we waited.
In the phosphorescent light, off towards shore,
we could see a figure crawling out on top of the rocks.
The lee of Fiddler's Green
gave him some shelter from the surf,
a shadow risking his life for strangers.
When he got as close as he dared,
he made several attempts to throw us a line
and finally succeeded.
I secured it to the mainmast
and the shadowed figure worked his way back ashore.
The four men grabbed the line and hauled it taunt
but the churning surf tossing and slamming us
defied the most courageous efforts of men
and great gaps of slack made the rope unstable.
The rescue effort was suspended.
They signaled and shouted to release their rope;
Eddie crawled forward and untied it from the mast.
We were left alone, untethered to earth,
striving to stay alive inside a nightmare of destruction.
Prisoners of a pounding sea to starboard
and jagged surf-battered rocks to port.

22.

Eddie, ever alert, fearless, poised to act
should the need arise. He never faltered.
My love and respect for him grew that night
as he proved himself to be
all any man could want in a shipmate
when the murderous night screams, *Hell!*
The power and fury in the heart of death
and destruction were awesome
and we were awed.
Sofia and Julie, without panic,
were emotionally expressive.
Sitting on the bunk in the wheelhouse
they huddled together giving each other comfort,
following my every movement with their eyes
telling me the onus was on me
to save them from this violent death.
As Fiddler's Green lifted with each new breaking wave
they would lift up from the wheelhouse bunk
and come down hard with a look of surprise
as my boat crashed hard on the rocks.
As for me?
In that night of pounding seas
from early dark to violent dawn,
with its surf, its rocks, its bloody shoals,
I did not weep and wail,
but cursed Death's violence
and trusted in my immortal soul.
In that night of wretched jostling,
with my worldly treasures lost,
dreams that had possessed my heart
became a thing now far apart.
I experienced a metamorphosis in my soul,
a transition from owner of a big yacht
to a penniless, homeless, vagabond of sorts.

23.

A dark and heavy albatross
seemed to take flight from my spirit,
as freedom from possessions left me free
to be once again a dreamer
running before the wind after Paradise;
and I vowed I would leave no unfilled desires
to anchor my soul on earth;
for I know the stuff dreams are made of.
The air heavy with cold night dew,
I looked at my young and healthy crew
and engraved in my heart a treasure still
of laughter and joy and a dream fulfilled.
They had become a part of the fabric of my life
and their love and laughter
would be there to greet me
whenever I sailed to that place far beyond.
The pounding surf kept slamming us
and shredding the bottom made of wood.
Every crashing wave cast us about
and slightly closer to shore.
The moon in its orbit ruling the tide
receded enough by dawn to decide
to leave us almost high and dry.

24.

Once again the four Mexicans arrived
and once again we secured the line.
First went Eddie to test it out.
He slipped and fell between the rocks,
the men on shore tightened their grasp
and that worn hemp line proved to be true.
Slipping, crawling and climbing
Eddie pulled himself ashore.
Sofia went next, followed by Julie,
and I was the last to say my good-byes
to the flotsam and jetsam of Fiddler's Green.

25.

We were led up the face of the cliff,
at times being lifted and pulled,
or crawling on all fours.
It was steep and arduous
with sharp rocks that shredded my boat shoes.
At the top was a fishing camp
consisting of a few tar paper shelters
and a one room dirt floor cabin
with a pickup truck parked in front.
The cabin belonged to the fifth man,
Mario, the boss,
his wife, and two small children.
He had not come down the cliff with the others.
His responsibility was in keeping it together,
telling the fishermen and his wife what to do.
We were tired cold, wet and hungry.
We sat on the ground. Leaned against the cabin,
and let the warmth of the sun heal us.
Mario told his wife to fix us some food.
His two small children peeked
from behind mama and stared at us.
We began to dry out. I let go of the horror,
and a tired peace engulfed me,
The warm feeling of the sun
filled my heart with gratitude. I smiled.

26

The small children came out and served us
with cups of fresh hot coffee.
My life force started to rise.
Next came Mama
with plates of huevos rancheros and beans.
Then the kids with hot tortillas and more coffee.
My senses started coming alive;
There was activity in my brain;
thoughts could recognize problems.
What are the possibilities of salvage?
Will Mario give us a ride to Ensenada?
I had a $500 money order and no cash.
I strolled to the edge of the cliff.
Looked down at the wreckage of Fiddler's Green
and I saw the potential for salvage.
I discussed the salvage with Eddie
and he agreed to take charge.
Bring everything salvageable to the top.
He would get the fishermen to help him.
I would go to San Diego
and come back with a pickup.
Then I negotiated a ride to Ensenada
for Sophia, Julie and myself,
and a twenty dollar cash loan,
bus fare for the three of us to the border.
The girls rode in the back of the pickup.
I sat up in front with Mario
and tried to remember the way we went.
There was no road. Only cattle paths
climbing up and running down over rocks,
twisting, bumping, turning,
forks in the paths to confuse.
Makeshift gates to open and close.
After thirty miles on the path we reached the highway.
Mario dropped us off at the bus station.

27.

I bought three tickets to Tijuana.
We walked through Customs to the highway.
The moment of our parting was upon us.
Their eyes glistened with tears,
their lips trembled with a deep sigh.
I told them,
"I know the stuff that dreams are made of.
They lie dormant in my imagination
Waiting to be born and given breath.
There is a never-ending path ahead.
There are shoals and hills are steep.
Sometimes you can't hang on
and slide back down,
but if you know with truth in your heart,
you are the stuff of dreams
then you get up and keep on climbing."

With a tender hug and a soft kiss
we said goodbye.
They smiled, stuck out their thumbs,
a car stopped immediately
and they disappeared from my view
to settle in the memories of my heart.

SAN DIEGO

1.

A shipwrecked sailor in a big city.
I didn't know a soul
and nary a soul wanted to know me.
I had a five hundred dollar money order,
but no bank knew me.
To be homeless, friendless, penniless,
and exhausted in a strange city
is to experience, *I Am*.
Only days past the equinox
the night moved in cold black.
Walking aimlessly I found life
in the trees and bushes of a small park.
I found my place in the bushes
and laid my head down on the cool earth,
surrendering to the indescribable
magnitude and majesty of the night sky.
I experienced the miracle of life
gathering strength from the earth and sky
renewing itself.
The burning light of the morning sun
brought me back to earth.
I arose and took a bearing.
I was on a hillside looking westward
toward an ever-expanding ocean.
To the southwest tall buildings.
I checked the wind direction
and pissed with the wind.
I stoked the inner fire
and walked toward the tall buildings.
At the first telephone
I made a collect call
to a sailor's kind of girl;
a Sweetheart who knows
a sailor's longing to be free.

How he'll love you when he meets you,
as he'll love you when he leaves you,
Fortunately, for me, she chose to be loving.
She was able to transfer five hundred
from her bank to one in San Diego.
I sent her my five hundred dollar money order.
I bought a local newspaper.
The choice of used pickups
I could afford was One.
A twenty-year old half-ton beat up Chevy.
It took two days for the registration
and to ready it with mind and the inner fire
for the trip south.

2.

Back at Punta San Jose
a forlorn-looking Eddie greeted me.
He had made a pile of salvage
and set up camp
in, on and around the pile.
It was his domain on Punta San Jose.
He ate and slept on the pile
retreating among the boulders
to find a place to squat in private.
The dregs of Fiddler's Green
made up the pile.
Eddie proclaimed
it was the best that he could do.
When I asked him about various items
He shrugged with, "I don't know."
Some gringo scavengers
offered to buy the Perkins engine
for two hundred dollars
where it sat in the rocks.
I accepted the deal.
The salvage was driven by scavengers.
They spotted the wreck,
and the shipwrecked sailor,
battered and bloodied.
From a hive out of nowhere they swarmed,
Landing on her carcass like hungry vultures.
It was a time like no other
and I knew in that instant
why the dead don't look back..
Thus the flesh was picked from my bones,
stripped naked, her ribs exposed,
she laid shattered and dead
on the rocks, still part of my mind.
I committed my spirit to rise,
driven by madness and the inner fire,
now a damp and seething ember in my heart:
So long as this body obeys this mind,

I will move forward from this flotsam and jetsam
and breathe a new beginning.
Yes, even in the maze of my mind.
Crawling from the sea, over the rocks,
alive with new life, I knew.
If the grave would know me,
let it know I persevered unto death.
Let the fire of passion consume it all.
Eddie helped me load
some of the remaining salvage.
We loaded that Chevy pickup
until the springs strained
and the front end tilted up.
I would take the load to San Diego,
find a place to store it, do a turn around
and come back for the final load and Eddie.

3.

The trip out for an old pickup
loaded beyond its half ton capacity
was done with the fire of passion.
Rocks and gullies.
Hills going down and up.
On one particularly steep grade the old Chevy
coughed out her heart and quit.
I tried and tried, but she didn't have the guts.
At the bottom of the hill I parked.
Piece by piece I unloaded the salvage
and on my back I trucked it
to the top of the hill.
Up and down I trudged that hill.
Sweat poured off me.
My breath labored.
My heart pounded in my chest
and in my ears:
"O, you mighty gods, I defy you.
If you think you can turn me into a quitter
with your obstacles and barricades,
you can kiss my ass!"
I added oil to the engine.
Backed her up as far as possible,
then giving her full throttle
I ran hard for the hill, hit the summit,
exhaled with a sigh and breathed a deep peace.
I reloaded the pickup,
then drove on singing,
"I was born one morning
when the sun didn't shine.
I picked up my back and walked to the sea.
I loaded a ton and a half of salvage and dreams.
And the scavengers said,
you poor dumb soul."

4.

By the time I reached Ensenada
the pickup had used five quarts of oil.
Then I saw a sign that beckoned me:
QUATRO HERMANOS, MECANICOS.
I inquired about a ring job, the cost and time.
They said they could do it in two hours
for eighty-five dollars, American.
I left the pickup.
Within a block I found tacos carnitas
and a cold cerveza.
Life is so beautiful. I smiled satisfied.
The four brothers proved true.
The only glitch was
one of them forgot
to tighten down the bolts on the oil pan.
Twenty miles down the road
I noticed a dangerous drop in oil pressure.
On the side of that Mexican highway
while lying on my back
grinning like a madman
I corrected the least of my problems.

5.

At the border the US Customs waited,
and wondered at this aging pickup
overloaded with flotsam and jetsam,
a red-eyed, glassy-eyed, crazy driver
talking gibberish about a shipwreck
racing with the sun and earth in orbit.
They wanted none of the confusion
that might interrupt the orderly
performance of their duties,
and they hastened me through
to be on my way.
On my way where? San Diego?
I had no place to store the salvage.
The attitude of the inhabitants
was one of caution
and, *"What's in it for me?"*
Finally I settled with a hardball dude
and the use of his sideyard
in exchange for part of the salvage.
Provided I took no longer than three days.
The white man didn't come to these shores
to find inner peace among the natives.
No, he came for material gain
and no crime nor scam was beneath him
to satisfy his lust and greed.
He has no soul brothers
and his treaties are without honor.

6.

Less than a day later I was back in Punta San Jose.
In my one day of absence
the pile had shrunk.
I wondered,
did he get a fair price for what he sold?
Even if my Spanish had been perfect
I doubt if Eddie would have told me why.
It was a time of survival for all hands
and why waste my time in anger?
Eddie and I loaded the pickup
with the last of the salvage.
I intended to take Eddie to Santa Cruz
where my connection could put him to work.
At the border the Border Patrol said, "No way."
I dug in my pocket
took out all the cash I had
and gave Eddie everything
but the gas money.
He was richer by far
than when he joined me in Mazatlan
and I hope much wiser.
The next couple of years were spent
mostly in Santa Cruz,
where the populace is in therapy
trying to build a new life
on the compost of old regrets.
Dysfunctional people abound there
but to me the whole world is dysfunctional;
or is that just a madman's perception?

A SAILING OFFER ACCEPTED

I did a boat delivery to Puerto Vallarta
with a retired dentist
and a couple of important rich kids.
Being rich gave them a sense of power
and they expected the kiss-up
as their inalienable right.
Their chatter did sound important
even though I couldn't make sense of it.
I saw it all laid out. A life one day long.
They would not experience in their heart
what singin' the Blues is all about,
their eyes never washed with tears,
or hearts never ablaze with fire.
In the quiet dark of the night
I rolled in the rockabye with the song of the sea
sounding on the hull sliding up and down.
Then the power of the sea grew mightier.
I remember 0300,
south of the Tropic of Cancer,
the dentist woke me.
Twenty foot swells were boring down on us.
He wanted my experience on the wheel.
I unfolded a bit of quality blotter
and washed it down with hot coffee.
I was at one with the blackness and the sea.
Red clouds came racing with the dawn
like Roman Legions hell-bound for thrills
and I had that boat driving with the swells,
rooster tails flying from her stern.
It was a time to remember
when the embers smolder in my heart.

A NITE IN THE CAN
November 1974, Santa Cruz

It started innocently enough.
We had worked hard for a congressional candidate,
an art professor with a speech impediment.
The day of the election we planned
a trip to Democratic Headquarters in Watsonville
where we'd listen to the returns.
And I had the day to idle away with my buddy, Doyle,
who also happened to be an art professor.
In our extended artistic family
we were always open to expanding our imaginations.
In the early afternoon some LSD was offered to us.
We thanked the donor, dropped it
and moved into a cosmic perception.
Later we discovered the herb cannabis
was very compatible with our space.
When the time came around to
travel to the Democratic Headquarters
and listen to the returns
Doyle and I were in a perfect, perfect high.
Being high with a soul brother
is one of those born-again experiences. However,
misfortune awaited us at the Headquarters
in the form of a free bar where our good friends
John and Bruce were the bartenders
with an attitude of it being sinful
to hold an empty glass.
The LSD and the Cannabis were fine with my mind
ah, but that alcohol destroyed my common sense.
Going home I put the pedal to the metal
in that old '53 Chevy pickup of mine,
even managed to break the speed limit
going down a long hill.
Then the cops got on my tail,
and that's how I spent a nite in the can.

ON THE ROAD AGAIN

I took off in the old blue pickup
hauling a travel-trailer to Arcata
for a horticulturist who wanted to study at Humbolt
and learn how to cultivate
psychedelic mushrooms.
I lingered awhile and met a professor,
working on a PhD in an organized life.
We did the mating dance
but couldn't keep in step.
She was happy with the sound of the surf
by the edge of the sea in a beautiful place
where the years would flow with the seasons.
One might enter a deep sleep,
awaken in the end and see only
a life grown old in a pot. Locked in.
As for me, I saw faraway places
in the inner light of the western sun.
They gripped my heart with a hunger
to experience the diversity of people
in all the colors they are known.

THE NORTHWEST

From Arcata I went to Ashland, Oregon
and earned a few bucks putting
in a hardwood floor.
Then moved on to Seattle
where I met a man and woman
traveling around in a Volkswagen van.
They had simplified their lives
by harvesting weeds, juicing them
and drinking the juice.
They were disciples of Ann Wigmore
who ran Hippocrates Health Institute in Boston.
Annie advocated sprouts
and wheat-grass juice
as the perfect diet and cure-all.
Simple.
Ideal for the cruising life, I thought,
and headed for Boston to learn more.

THE NORTHEAST

Boston, the old hometown was proper cold.
Even in the middle of summer.
I joined the staff at Hippocrates.
The diet was a bore
but among the staff and guests
there was peace, joy and love.
I took an older beauty to Cambridge
for a walk in Longfellow Park.
With yoga and diet she worked hard
at staying ahead of age and decay.
Her options were disappearing.
She had an architect in New York on hold.
There was no great love for him
but he could afford her.
There I met Diana.
Fair of form and pleasant in disposition.
We kept in touch.

RETURN TO SANTA CRUZ

I started a health food store
on a borrowed five thousand
from a wannabe capitalist
who knew all the wrong answers
cemented in his closed mind.
Six months later it ended up
me giving the business
to my dysfunctional kids.
They turned it into a dysfunctional business.
Diana joined me for a month or two
and we played at being lovers.
My heart was in a world cruise.
She asked me one day,
"What's the most important thing to you?"
"A world cruise. Why?"
Diana's heart was not in the endless sea
but in an acre or two.
She packed her cat,
loaded her Volkswagen Bug
and left looking for a place to make a life.
It took me awhile to figure out
how I blew it.
I had much to learn about loving womankind.
But I knew the cure for a lonely rejected heart,
Love. Love again.

SPENDING MY TIME

All my life I'd strain through pain
For the love of living life.
There never was a job I couldn't do
once I put my mind to it.
I never did learn to work for a living.
Living, I felt, was a gift from the Everlasting.
There never was a job I couldn't walk away from,
and I would do so with a will,
because it is my life in time space.
My time is a priceless treasure.
What drove me down the road,
was the hungering in my heart
to experience the whole of it.
I worked best when I was
totally possessed by the inner fire,
with my heart as the guide
living in the moment.
When you strip away all dogma and philosophy
standing naked and alone, cold
or sweating in the fields,
all you ever really have
from conception to the grave
is a passage in time.
I must be free to live and love
with all my heart this time around.
The power of decision is mine
and I think it is better to try and fail
than never to have tried at all.
Regrets at the end of time are bitter pills.

ODYSSEY

Once I treasured great material wealth
but I found all material wealth was subject to
theft, taxes, rot, decay, and shipwreck.
And of course those fair weather
friends and relatives feasting
on whatever they might garnish from
your bounty
were happy to tolerate your company,
if there was something in it for them,
while they looked forward to your demise.
I wanted something more, something eternal.
I went in search of Fiddler's Green, Nirvana.
Traveling through the Apocalypse of my soul
I was guided by the wisdom of my heart
and in the crucible I found compassion, understanding
and the God of Love.

A WANDERING STRAY

1.

It was the summer of '76.
I'd gone to Seattle on a boat delivery.
I knew a couple of professors there,
a sociologist and an anthropologist
who were both connoisseurs of fine herbal highs.
I enjoyed their company.
I also enjoyed my own company.
I was at a place in my life
where I had my time
and was free to spend my time
wondering and wandering
in the faraway dimensions of my mind,
or traveling to fantasy land
where I might learn the secret of
having my desires blossom and bear fruit.
In the embers of my heart simmered desire
to know what bliss the Everlasting
might bestow upon this consciousness of mine.
Why not? According to Moses
I was created by God in God's image and likeness.
Like Jesus, I could say with sincerity,
"All that my father has is mine."
Thus, o thus, a night of laughter,
a sunset, a sunrise over Bombay,
the sound of the city coming alive,
the smell, the stink and the fumes,
living the cycle of life,
birthing and dying.
I was ever a vagabond,
only because I was a dreamer
and would settle for nothing less
than Nirvana, or Fiddler's Green,
I took inventory:
I knew that mind was the Master Power
and I was mind.

I knew how to fast, to meditate.
I knew that thoughts are things
and my mind was filled with great thoughts.
I looked upon my health as being slightly
above average,
albeit I received a small monthly stipend
for having been diagnosed with MS.
But I knew the stuff that dreams are made of.
The early evening of July 8th
found me at the Deluxe One on North Broadway,
a two-day growth on my chin,
a buck seventy-five in my pocket,
running politically incorrect verse by
a black broadcast journalist,
looking forward to my check in the morning.
I had an empty beer glass in my hand.
The night had nothing to offer
but to go back to that squalid room and read.
Then out of the smoke and the laughter
a Mona Lisa appeared through the haze,
full of bosom, narrow of waist,
broad of hip, sturdy of thigh,
and an eye that said,
"My love flows steady as the Mississippi."
She had a pitcher of beer
and was eating away at a salad.
I only glanced at her,
yet she caught my eye and held it
while she seared my soul
with promises of her warm and tender body
engulfing all of me.
"Can I fill your glass? I have a whole pitcher."
"Why not?"
And we met ... strangers no more.
I asked because I really wanted to know:
"What do you want out of life?"
"That's a strange question,
I suppose everything. Why?"
"How'd you like to start with a world cruise,
maybe sail all the way to Paradise?"

"I'd love to. How?"
"I'm a sailor and a boat builder
and I know the stuff that dreams are made of."
And that day I was born again
when she bought into my dream,
and the sum of the parts
became greater than the parts,
and the birth of my dream began to quicken.
I experienced the thrill of flight with the speed of light,
of dancing in the clouds with the gods,
of the inner fire glowing hot
consuming the dross and regrets
from the dead past of all my life.
To be near her, to touch her hand,
caused my heart to overflow with bliss-
it had that warmth that only love knows.

2.

We honeymooned on the Washington coast.
We had a tube tent, a sleeping bag,
and seventy pounds of watermelon, in season.
Our breathing took on the rhythm of the waves
coming in and going out like the sands of time
erasing the past and leaving a new beginning.
Above us a universe of stars told tales
of infinity and never-ending bliss
as we snuggled close for warmth and love.
After a week we headed south
and we slept out every night
wherever we might be,
but always under the protective sight
and trust in the God of Love.

3.

I was but a wandering poet/dreamer
captivated by the warm and tender charms
of the feminine form, voice and mind.
My Beloved is a natural born teacher.
When my mind is open she fills it;
when my mind is closed she ignores it.
Having sailed and loved in the four winds
and the seven seas I was worldly wise
in the ways to a woman's heart.
I pleaded with her to teach me more
if there was more to learn.
She found me sincere and worthy of teaching.
Forthwith began my learning
of the finer points and the hidden points
in the beautiful and mysterious places
lovers can express themselves
in loving their beloved, where the juices of love
mingle and flow to experience the bliss
together, as one being.
I learned, willingly I learned.
I learned to get it right.
And together we learned and grew.

HOLLISTER AND SANTA CRUZ

We found an old ranch house in Hollister
fifty miles southeast of Santa Cruz.
It was a four hundred acre ranch with cattle,
a walnut orchard, and an apricot orchard.
It had a great stone fireplace
and some convenient trees to swing a hammock.
The rent was only $ 85.00 per month, a bargain,
but the house was dirty and in disrepair
without bed, or other furnishings.
We worked together and in a few weeks,
had not a house, but a home.
I was awed by Betty Jean's competence and genius
in turning that shack into a comfortable palace.
Blessed is the man who has a strong,
independent and free partner for a wife.
It was too late in the year to start a garden,
but she laid it out for spring.
Of all the gifts in life I have ever been given
there is none that compares to Betty Jean.
In Hollister I would greet the morning sun
and shout out to God,
"Thank you God, for Betty Jean."
Life and living can often be hard and difficult,
and we can pay for our mistakes
time and time again.
But, how sweet it is
when one has a loving partner.
Side by side we worked building our boat.
Betty Jean learned how to handle the tools
and do all of the things that I had already known.
She was not just an assistant partner, and sweetie,
she gave her own creative input
that contributed greatly to the warmth
of our scene.

During those days the MS was all but forgotten
except for painful spasticity in my upper back.
The ideal treatment is marijuana.
It has none of the side effects
found in traditional prescription medicine.
We were fortunate to have friends
coming by to look at the progress on our boat,
many of them would share a smoke,
and my spasticity would find temporary relief.
The medical profession tried to legalize marijuana
for people with MS
but unfortunately the courts refused the request.
After having looked at the scientific information
and the misinformation on marijuana,
I have to conclude that the corporate giants
in liquor and pharmaceuticals
must have the power to keep the herb illegal.
It is too easily grown in any back yard.
Or maybe the secret government
is aware that the deceit
that supports the Baloney Curtain
is threatened because smokers often
question authority.
Our boat we decided to call the 'Sweetie'.
To have a Sweetie, one must be a Sweetie.
It was a thirty-one foot trimaran
with an eighteen and one half foot beam.
From Hollister to the harbor in Santa Cruz
was fifty miles and I thought the permits
from the bureaucracy would be well-nigh impossible.
I wanted to design some method
of bolting on the pontoons at the harbor.
It could have resulted in a weak link
in the overall construction of the boat.
From far port to far starboard
one piece construction was the strongest.
Betty Jean undertook the problem of permits
and to my astonishment she succeeded.
We continued building without fear of a weak link.
Betty Jean and I had been living in Hollister

and working on the Sweetie for a year.
We had been together for a total of fourteen months.
I was happy in that farmhouse,
loving and working with her.
I knew a deep inner peace and joy.
If God can offer me as much in the Promised Land
it will please my soul.
Early September of '77 we decided
it was time to move the Sweetie to Santa Cruz.
Betty Jean had all the permits in order.
I rented a Ditch Witch trailer
that was much too short for the job.
Transferring the boat from cradle to trailer
was only marginally difficult,
but jockeying the borrowed pickup
and boat-loaded trailer through the ranch
and down the farm road was extremely difficult
and hazardous.
I had a few high tense moments
when I almost took a power pole down.
Betty Jean turned white but kept her cool.
Through some city streets, down a freeway,
through some more city streets, a country road,
and finally, a boat yard in Santa Cruz.
We secured the boat.
It was now time for me to be introduced
to Betty Jean's mom and dad in Arkansas.
We headed east and made the rounds
where I met the in-laws and cousins.
Most all of them were good solid stock
from the kind of people who had built America.
I was warmly and graciously received,
even though considered a bit far out,
but poets in the heartland of America
are usually oddball strangers...
and especially ones from California.
When we returned to Santa Cruz
the rainy season was upon us
and the Sweetie was not quite ready to move aboard.
We shared an apartment with another couple,

did what work we could on the Sweetie,
and odd jobs to supplement our income.
In February of '78 we moved aboard.
She was still in the boatyard
but it gave Betty Jean and me our own space
to play and snuggle.
When the whole concept of this world cruise
was first conceived in my imagination
I considered writing a 'how to' book on it.
It was to be called, "Low Budget Cruising."
The lesson I had learned from Fiddler's Green
and how opulence separates one from real people
was one I did not want to have to repeat.
The yacht club set held no appeal for me
with their factitious friendliness
and self importance.
I much preferred the company of fishermen.
An important part of the low budget cruising technique
is how to eat an inexpensive diet, easy to prepare,
that is both tasty and healthy.
Grains, beans, and seeds, when sprouted,
offer endless possibilities of meeting
the requirements of such a diet.
The cockpit of the Sweetie was our living area.
It was eight feet long covered with an awning.
Settees on port and starboard sides
could seat eight on foam cushions.
A table with a large drop leaf, when opened,
provided space for guests.
The wheel was mounted on the forward bulkhead,
and the helmsman could sit on the table.
We actually entertained guests for dinner
in the boatyard, aboard the Sweetie.
They were very pleasurable and memorable dinners.
Our date to launch was May 31st, 1978,
less that two years from meeting my mate
with whom I wish to wander this earth
and perhaps the universe.

MY BELOVED

My Beloved gave birth to my heart.
During the day going our separate ways,
she is the reason I desire to be
worthy of love.
She is the reason I breathe.
And if the gods wanted her to breathe no more
I would plead that they take me to my last breath.
To give my life for her would please me.
In searching for Fiddler's Green
I was searching for Nirvana,
much as mind might desire the Holy Grail.
I wanted the experience; it was very necessary
to burn, blissfully to burn,
consumed in orgasm.
Give me this and I will die for you.
It is my reason for being committed to Being,
Loving my Beloved.
This thing called love is the path to the Eternal.
I stay on the path and my love grows.
It grows and it glows brighter,
it just keeps growing and glowing.
I float in its warmth, caressed,
One with my Beloved, souls united.
And the bliss grows with it,
for the sum of the parts
is greater than its parts.
Then, all that I am
is in orgasm with Creation
and I see with my heart,
as I drink deep from the Holy Grail,
Love is the Force
that gives the atom its spin,
Creation its reason for Being.

WALKING THE TALK

We went on a boat delivery
from Santa Cruz to San Francisco Bay.
It was a small gaff-rigged sloop
with a one-lunger diesel for auxiliary.
We left at night and would arrive at dawn.
There was no wind and the ocean was like glass.
The stars reflected their light
on the dark surface of the sea.
Fish darting alongside
created streaks of bright phosphorous.
Gently, ever so gently, the Pacific swells
rolled under that little sloop
and rocked it just about right
for totally letting go.
And my lady love retched out her guts
all the windless and peaceful long night.
Hours after she had regurgitated everything
she was hanging over the gunnel dry heaving.
In that night with the engine chug-chugging along
I knew that if I was to know happiness
it would be only through the joy of my lady-love
for my heart rejoiced in her joy. I knew her pain.
I had given her my heart.
From that day on I have been her love slave,
and it is the sweetest gig I've ever had.

MY GODDESS
For Betty Jean at the beginning of a new millennium

You are the reason I live,
the reason I breathe.
With laughter and joy I live and breathe
for I feel in my heart the joy of your joy,
and I overflow with the ecstasy
of serving you, love,
throughout the days and nights of all my life.
This flesh of mine dissolves
in pulsating waves of
magnetic anti-gravity repulsing all but love.
Then an all encompassing power of the Everlasting
bathes me in the warm light of love.
In that Spiritual Instant I know:
where two or more are gathered together
in Love's name there is the God of Gods.
Truly, I believe that I am richer
than any man on earth,
for I walk and talk with the Gods.

SATURDAY MORNING IN NIRVANA
Summer, 1999

Up in time to order the sun to rise
and with the sun over my shoulder
sitting in a comfortable chair
facing Mystic Mountain
the waters of Infinity Falls
sing their song in the quiet of
the dawn's early light.
Thinking, meditating, wondering
about the meaning of life,
the reason for being.
I'm enjoying a good book
joined by my beloved,
with the sweetness of growing things
providing a privacy curtain
of bright blossoms and green life.
We breathe deep and inhale the flowers,
the smoky mist rises and disappears,
the sun lights the earth,
the Goddess secretes her nectar
and we merge into total oneness
beyond, beyond.
Time and space fade in glory
and I am in orgasm with the universe.
Love expressing Itself inspires awe,
a blissful kind of awe,
where you go to the edge of consciousness
and then jump over into the unknown
and there you are, you and your muse, One.
Where do we go from here?

A HIGHER POWER

I let go of ego self.
A higher power enters me.
My heart overflows
and I tell my goddess,
I adore her.
My heart thrills
with the wonder of Love.

CONSUMED

When passion stirs her soul she beckons me.
I approach her.
Gently she engulfs me.
Softly presses against me.
Her heat is compounded by mine.
She smiles and softly moans with pleasure
as she gives me the gift of her sweet juices.
In the fire of her passion she is demanding
the totality that is me.
She will settle for nothing less.
I let go with a will and surrender
with every heartbeat and breath
I surrender all that I am.
Her entire being and essence
feed in ecstasy
as my life force fills her.
Then she smiles
and laughs a happy laugh.
I feel like the black widow's mate,
digested and no regrets.
I rest in peace beyond understanding.

A HORSE IN A CORRAL

She was a white solitary horse
in a big old corral.
About the middle of the corral
was a lone power pole.
That lonely old horse
wore a smooth place on that power pole
where she nuzzled it hour upon hour.
Pretending it was one of her kind.

She was one lonely old horse.

COMMIT YOUR HEART AND MIND
TO THIS:

"Learn to love,
the lesson is but plain;
and once made perfect
is never lost again."

Shakespeare

MAX

I had just gotten out of my pickup on Front Street.
A kid about nine sticks this ball of fur at me;
I had no choice but to catch it.
"Hey, mister, want a puppy?"
If his breed had a name it would be Raggety Mutt.
First thing that guy did was start licking me
like I'm the love of his life.
And that was how
Marvelous Max the Magnificent, the Canine Cannonball,
came to be my tutor.

He looked like a dirty grayish black mop lying on the floor.
But when it came to the ladies
he was all Don Juan.

I introduced him to my Beloved, Betty Jean.
"Honey, meet Max."
She said, "O, no, we don't need a dog."
That didn't stop Max.
He went to work on Betty Jean
with wagging tail and licking tongue.

I laid back and watched
as that dumb mutt turned my Beloved
into his care giver and servant.
She would bathe him and rub him dry,
trim his toenails, pick up his mess,
pick out his fleas, cut his hair,
see that he was warm and dry
and well fed.
When he needed a vet she paid the bill.

When she came through the door
after a tiring day in the classroom,
Max would greet her like a Goddess.
He would overwhelm her with his joy.
I watched these developments with apprehension.
Max was moving in on my position as Top Dog!

I started to imitate Max,
and when my Beloved came through the door
we both raced to greet her.
I put my arms around her,
I put my lips on hers,
and while Max yelped at being ignored,
I was telling her I loved her.

It didn't stop there
because Max was a snuggler,
and every chance he'd get
he'd snuggle up with my Beloved.
He was becoming the top dog for snuggling.
Ah, but I had an advantage
because I had two hands and two arms,
and whenever I saw the opportunity
of hugging and snuggling my Sweetheart
I put my hands and arms to work.

Seeing what made Max so lovable
helped me to move forward as a lover,
capable of intense joy at the mere presence of my Beloved,
in just being who she is deep inside,
where the real person resides,
free to be, whether in denim or silk.
But once I did,
and experienced how much I'd been missing,
I thanked Max for showing me the fine art of
Communicating Love.

KEYS TO THE KINGDOM

Love will always act
with the happiness and well-being
of the beloved in the forefront
of every day's
need to put a meal on the table
or fix a hole in the roof.
When two or more are gathered together
in Love's name
the sum of the parts is greater than the parts.
It is there one can experience bliss.
Without the experience bliss is unknown.
Without love bliss is unknown.

Love is awesome.
God is Love.
Love is the gateway to immortality.
Like the universe, Love has no boundaries.

What things are they that Love is made of?
I saw a picture of starving children in the Sudan.
A starving baby in its starving mother's arms.
I saw a picture of children, small children
scavenging in the dumps of Jakarta.
My heart aches and that is the pain of Love.
To send them food, not bombs
that is the manifestation of Love.
Love isn't Love
until you give it away.

To know Love as well as Love knows you
can carry a person to a place
where the light of knowledge
and the warmth of Love
are all encompassing.

What can I do with Love?
Can I spend it at the Food Mart?
Can it buy a Lear jet?
You can Love yourself
with your whole heart and soul.

Once you Love yourself totally
you will have limitless love
to give away.
As long as you keep giving it
Love will never dry up.

How sweet it is to wash clean the mind
of all those things that block Love:
guilt, sin, anger, condemnation and fear.
All those things that are the opposite of Love
in whose shadow Love cannot be known.

How sweet it is to experience the totality of Love
in your own heart.
To feel your heart overflow with Love
and all you can do is give it away.
Loving and being Lovable are absolute.

When you are loving
you are lovable.
That is an eternal truth.

In the very essence of Love there is compassion ...
Love is very, very compassionate.

Love is quick to forgive.
Forgiveness can open the door
to give and receive Love.

Love doesn't hold grievances,
and yet it will give all that it has,
even its own life,
if it will stop crimes against humanity.

To know real joy, bliss that keeps expanding,
learn to love.
To learn the things that Love is made of,
is to experience Love with the totality of your being.
How beautiful and sweet it is.

To Love with your heart, your soul, your spirit,
is to know beyond a doubt that:
I Love, therefore I am.

Much of what people think they know about Love
isn't worth knowing:
"I love you because you're my mother."
"I love you because I gave birth to you."

Love is not Love when preceded by conditions:
"If you don't go to bed this minute
I'll stop loving you."
"I'd love him if he'd buy me a diamond ring."

I have one mind
and that mind I share with Love.
Love is in everything I see
because Love is in my heart and mind.

How will I know when I really love another?
When that person's happiness and well-being
takes precedence over my own.
For in their happiness and well-being,
I can experience Love.

The nature of Love is to extend Itself ...
The nature of the Universe is to expand.
It is the nature of Love to grow and glow ...
First one must learn to give it away.
To know Love the experience is necessary.
One begins by making a commitment
to learn to love.

Love has no atomic structure ...
yet, it is what holds the atom together.
love acts as a counterforce to gravity,
the body often feels like it can walk on water
or fly without wings ...
like a light in the sky that zips here and there.
Those UFOs may be lovers uniting
dancing in the stars.
Love is without beginning
and Love is without end.
To experience Perfect Love
is indescribable bliss.
No chemicals, herbs, nor drugs
can bring one to this place of bliss.

When the atom is amplified many times
the observer sees more void than solids.
Science can't put love under a microscope.
To be Loving is the reason to be living.

Love is caring.
The end of life in a body is death.
The birth of immortality is learning Perfect Love
and giving it away.

When the body moves aside
Love moves into other dimensions.
It continues to grow and expand
to give the atom its spin.

If my Beloved needed a heart
I would give her mine.
Without a moment
of hesitation.

Living my life in search of the ultimate dream,
has, above all, been an experience.
But my consciousness is only aware
of what it has experienced.

There comes with the growth
a knowing that one has conquered
the life in a body
and is ready to begin again in other dimensions
ever closer to the Absolute.

EPITAPH
County Cork '69

Bury me deep where I'll serve love best,
loving you in my sleep
or with a rose rising from my breast.
But send no flowers and cry no tears,
for I've given my heart away through the years
and there's nothing left for Death to find
in a spiritless, heartless
shell of some kind.

WHO AM I

The studying and searching years of my life
I was a planetary rover, or a vagabondo du mar.
My consciousness has always needed the experience
to give what lies within my imagination
the texture of reality outside my imagination.
Even though I wrote those above lines
I have to follow them to know where they lead.
I am subject to bliss, the passion of madness,
and the abyss that follows the fall.
My soul rejoices with free thinkers.
I have no choice in the matter.
If I can't breathe free I suffocate.
I love, eat and fornicate,
but beyond it all, at the center,
at the summit of my being,
I have let go of this world,
gone deep within and glimpsed other dimensions.
The desire was there
but there was no plan, no chart, no map
that led me stumbling through the looking glass.
The way back to the dark was all downhill,
because Love spoils a man for all else.
I entered the Black Hole fully aware
it is death to all my days gone by,
the noise, the disharmony, the rot,
sleazy politicians and their power
to make and sell laws creating crimes.
I have gone beyond the dead past.
What was the garbage of my yesterdays
has entered the cosmic compost pile.
But there will come a time when I will be
all that the Everlasting intended me to be.

I wrote a long epic poem published in 1967.
It sold twenty thousand copies in the first release.
The publisher had printed fifty thousand copies
but would not fill orders after the first shipment.
It was politically and socially satirical.
I looked behind the Iron Curtain, the Bamboo Curtain
and then I looked behind the most powerful of all,
the one that messes with your mind,
the Baloney Curtain.
It's sort of like questioning authority;
the ruling powers don't like to be questioned.
They want to deny that without beginning
was the law, and the law was, Cause and Effect.
As you learn, so shall you know
the only constant is change.

Soon to be published by Love Extension Press:
TRUTH GOES ON TRIAL

If you are unable to find titles published by Love Extension Press at your local bookseller then contact the publisher at:

Love Extension Press
35 Holt Lane, Suite B
Chico, CA 95926

Or by phone at (530) 893- 4429
Fax (530) 893- 0902